Spock the Donkey

story by Jeremy Strong
illustrated by Steve Smallman

"Today we are going to visit the City Farm," said Mr Hopkins.

Miss Cherry smiled at Mouse and Jojo.
"We will see your mum when we get there."

Billy Steel laughed.
"Does your mum live at the farm?" he said.
"Don't be silly," said Mouse and Jojo.
"She works there."

The children walked to the farm.
They met Jojo and Mouse's mum.

At the farm there were cows and goats and sheep and hens and horses.

There was a donkey too.
He was called Spock.

Spock had big pointed ears.
"Spock likes apples,"
said Mrs Macdonald.

Mrs Macdonald forgot to shut the gate.

Spock pushed the gate with his nose.

He ran out.
"Oh no!" cried Mrs Macdonald.

"Catch that donkey!"
shouted Miss Cherry.
"Catch that donkey!"
shouted the children.

Spock ran round the farm.
He said *hello* to the hens.

He said *goodbye* to the cows.

He said *can't catch me* to the sheep and goats!

"We can catch you!" cried everyone.
They ran after the donkey.

Miss Cherry jumped onto his back.
Everyone cheered.

Miss Cherry rode Spock around the farm.

She rode him back.
Ben shut the gate.

"Thank you everyone.
You saved the day!" laughed
Mrs Macdonald.